Elite

EMBOSSING

Ina Scheurwater

FORTE PUBLISHERS

Contents

Fourth printing November 2003
ISBN 90 5877 207 1

This is a publication from
Forte Publishers BV
P.O. Box 1394
3500 BJ Utrecht
The Netherlands

For more information about the creative books available from Forte Uitgevers:
www.hobby-party.com

Publisher: Marianne Perlot
Editor: Hanny Vlaar
Photography and digital image editing: Fotografie Gerhard Witteveen, Apeldoorn, the Netherlands
Cover and inner design:
Studio Herman Bade BV, Baarn, the Netherlands

Preface

In my previous book, I wrote that you often get new ideas from the many attractive materials which appear on the market. The same is true for the **line embossing stencils**, which offer a great many possibilities. This time, the cards are stippled with stamp-pad ink. A big advantage with this method is that it dries quickly so that so can start cutting the card straight away. This book gives you eleven different possibilities, but I'm sure you will also come up with some great ideas yourself. After the holidays, I also hope to use these wonderful stencils in my workshops. Have fun!

Thanks
Firstly, Marianne, for having the faith to allow me to make this book. Also, the photographer Gerhard Witteveen, for the pleasant cooperation. And Mr. G. Nederlof from Oegstgeest, the Netherlands, who always willingly corrected my writing and returned it via e-mail.

Techniques

Embossing techniques

Secure the embossing stencil to the light box using adhesive tape. Next, place the card on the stencil with the good side facing the stencil and secure it in place using non-permanent adhesive tape. Turn the light on. First, gently push the embossing pen between the open lines and then push a little harder. Use the thin point for the really narrow lines. If the card needs to be stippled, do this before removing the card from the stencil.

Cut individual pieces out leaving a 2 mm border. Do this carefully and always rotate the paper whilst keeping the scissors still. Round off all the points to finish it off nicely.

Tip 1

It is easier to emboss using a smooth pen. You can use Pergasoft, a candle or dry toilet soap to make the pen smooth. You can also rub it on the places to be embossed.

Stippling with stamp-pad ink

Apply a small amount of ink to a foam brush or a small piece of sponge and rub this up and down the embossed lines.

1. Materials.

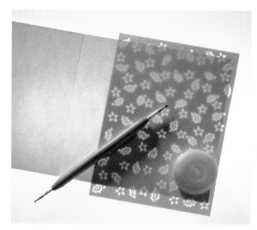

2. Emboss the background.

3. Emboss a winter rose and cut it out leaving a 2 mm border.

4. Emboss the centre of the winter rose and stipple the rose before removing the stencil from the paper.

Use a different brush or sponge for each colour. Tear thin paper into pieces and use them to cover the parts which must not be touched.

When you are finished, clean the stencil with a tissue.

Tip 2
Punch or pierce a hole in a piece of paper and use this to protect the rest of the card when stippling, for example, small sections, such as eyes or buttons.

Using the cutting templates
Copy the shapes (pages 19 and 22) onto the card using the light box. Photocopy the page if you find it difficult to use the book.

Tip 3
To make a border in coloured or white paper, cut a 2 mm opening in, for example, the back of a plastic cover. Allow the opening to protrude on both sides to see what has to be embossed. Embossing stencil no. 262 from Leane de Graaf is very useful.

Materials

- Card – Artoz (Kars)
- Frame cards (Romak)
- Christmas vellum (Kars)
- Line embossing stencils: LE 2401 to LE 2406 (Kars)
- Line embossing pen (Kars)
- Light box
- Stamp-pad ink
- Foam brushes or pieces of sponge
- Pergasoft or a candle
- Washi paper (brown and cream)
- Circle cutter
- Scribbles (gold)
- Glitter glue (transparent)
- Cutting mat
- Knife
- Ruler

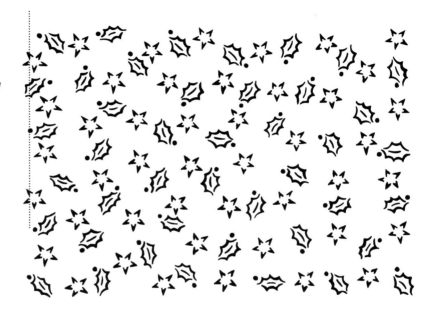

- Scissors
- Photo glue
- Adhesive tape
- Silicon glue
- Aleene's True Snow
- Organza ribbon (haberdashery shop)

Unless otherwise stated, the double cards are made from A5 sheets which have been folded double.

Specific materials are stated with each card.

Villages in the winter

The houses and the church

stand peacefully in

the winter landscape.

What you need:
- ❏ *Card: pastel blue no. 413*
- ❏ *Embossing paper: white*
- ❏ *Line stencil: LE 2402*
- ❏ *Stamp-pad ink: light brown and orange*

Card 1

Emboss two hills. Cut them out and stick the highest hill on the blue double card. Slightly bend the second hill and stick it on the card using a large drop of silicon glue. Stick the sides of the hill to the card. Emboss and stipple a church. Emboss and stipple the roof and the portal again and then only emboss and stipple the portal. Cut them out leaving a 2 mm border. Stick them on the card in 3D using small drops of silicon glue, so that the church is on the top hill . Emboss and stipple three different trees and cut them out. Bend them and position them at different heights on the hills. Emboss three different stars.

Cut them out and stick them on the blue part of the card using a small drop of silicon glue.

Card 2

Make a double card (12.5 x 12.5 cm). Emboss three different hills and cut them out leaving a 2 mm border. Stick the highest hill on the card using photo glue. Slightly bend the second and third hills and stick them on the card using a large drop of silicon glue. Stick both sides of the hills to the card. Emboss and stipple two houses. Emboss and stipple the roofs twice. Emboss and stipple a street light and three trees of different heights and cut them out. Slightly bend the trees and stick them on different hills on the card using silicon glue. Make the roofs of the houses 3D. Also position the houses at different heights. Use a cocktail stick to carefully bend the street light. Stick the top of the street light to the card using a drop of silicon glue and stick the bottom of the street light to the card using photo glue. Emboss three white stars. Cut them out and stick them on the blue part of the card using a small drop of silicon glue.

Card 3

The materials and the instructions are the same as for cards 1 and 2.

1.

2.

3.

Prettige
Feestdagen

Snowman

The snowman stands proudly outside and defies the freezing cold.

What you need:
- ❏ *Card: white no. 211, blue no. 427, wine red no. 519 and dark green no. 309*
- ❏ *Line stencils: LE 2403 and LE 2401*
- ❏ *Stamp-pad ink: black, brown, red, blue and yellow*
- ❏ *Aleene's True Snow*

Card 1

Cut out a strip of white card (7 cm wide). Emboss and stipple a snowman. Emboss and stipple a hat and a scarf on a scrap piece of card. Follow the instructions given for card 2. Make two small hills (see above). Add some snow using a cocktail stick. Stick everything on a red double card. Decorate the card with a gold border.

Card 2

Make a double card (landscape) and stick a 9 cm wide blue strip on it. First, emboss the lines of all three hills on a scrap piece of card. Do this again on another piece of scrap card for two hills and then on another piece of scrap card for one hill. Slightly bend them and stick them on top of each other using a large drop of silicon glue. Stick the left-hand and right-hand sides of the hills to the card. Emboss and stipple a bird table. Emboss and stipple the roof again and emboss and stipple two birds. Cut everything out leaving a 2 mm border. Raise the roof using silicon glue. Slightly bend the birds, place a drop of silicon glue behind them and stick them on the bird table. Emboss a snowman and stipple the eyes, buttons (see Techniques, tip 2), broom and nose. Emboss and stipple an extra hat and scarf on a scrap piece of card. Cut everything out. Slightly bend them and add a drop of silicon glue behind the hat and the scarf. Stick the snowman on the hills using a large drop of silicon glue. Use a cocktail stick to add snow to the hills, the bird table and the snowman.

Card 3

Cut a piece of green card (10.5 x 10.5 cm) and emboss a border around it (see Techniques, tip 3). Stick this on the front of a square double card

(12.5 x 12.5 cm). Cut a circle out of this (Ø 8 cm). Emboss and stipple a snowman on the inside of the double card, so that it is exactly in the middle of the circle. See the instructions given above to finish off the snowman. Emboss some trees and snowflakes around the snowman. Decorate the green part of the card with gold dots (scrap pieces from decorative borders).

1.

2.

3.

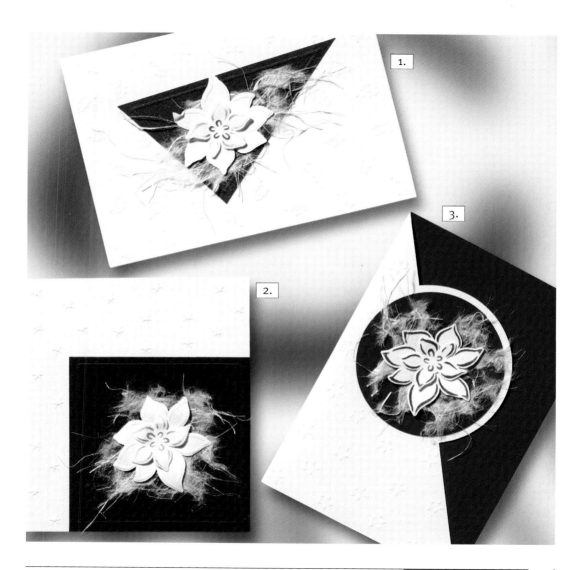

1.

3.

2.

Winter rose

It appears that

these winter roses are

lying in the snow.

What you need:
- ❏ *Card: white no. 211, dark green no. 309,*
  dark blue no. 417 and wine red no. 519
- ❏ *Line stencils*
- ❏ *Stamp-pad ink: green, silver and red*

Card 1

Line stencil nos: LE 2404 and LE 2406
Cut out a green triangle (see the template on page 22) and emboss a border 0.5 cm from the sides (see Techniques, tip 3). Use a pencil to indicate on the inside of the front of the double card where the triangle is to be positioned. Emboss the background around this shape. Stick the triangle on the card. Tear off some washi paper and stick this in the middle using photo glue. Emboss a winter rose and cut it out. Next, only emboss the centre of the rose. Stipple it with green ink and cut it out. Stick the winter rose on the card using one drop of silicon glue.

Bend the petals of the centre of the rose using a cocktail stick, place a drop of silicon glue behind them and stick them on the winter rose.

Card 2

Line stencils: LE 2401 and LE 2406
Use a square double card (12.5 x 12.5 cm) and a piece of blue card (8.5 x 8.5 cm). See the instructions given for card 1.

Card 3

Line stencils: LE 2404 and LE 2406
Stick half of a wine red card in a white portrait card. Use a pencil to draw a line from the top left-hand corner to the bottom right-hand corner of the card. Cut out a semicircle 3.5 cm from the top left-hand corner. Cut away the rest of the card along the diagonal line. Set the circle cutter to a slightly smaller size and cut a circle out of a scrap piece of wine red card. Use a pencil to indicate inside the front of the card where the circle is to be positioned and emboss the background around this shape. Stick the wine red circle on the front of the card. See the instructions given for card 1 to finish the card.

Windows

Look at the warmth

in the house or the winter

scenery outside.

What you need:
- ❏ *Card: wine red no. 519*
- ❏ *Romak frame cards*
- ❏ *Line stencil: LE 2406*
- ❏ *Stamp-pad ink: green, red, silver and light brown*
- ❏ *Glitter glue: transparent*

Card 1

Emboss some bricks around the window. If you do not have this stencil, you can easily make your own. Cut approximately five bricks out of dark coloured card or gold card and use this as a stencil. Stick half of a wine red card inside the card and decorate it with gold dots (scraps pieces from border stickers). Emboss and stipple some pine branches with berries and the centre of a winter rose. Cut them out leaving a 2 mm border. Slightly bend them, add a drop of silicon glue behind them and use them to make an attractive window decoration. If you wish, add some glitter glue. Finish the card with two toadstools.

Card 2

Emboss and stipple a bow (do the loops twice). Cut them out leaving a 2 mm border. Place some silicon glue between the loops and stick them above the window. Make a window decoration across the entire length of the card (see photograph). The card is finished in the same way as described for card 1. Stick half of a wine red card inside this card as well. Decorate the card with gold dots and, if you wish, add some glitter glue.

Card 3

Cut a circle (Ø 7 cm) out of wine red card (10 x 10 cm) and stick this inside the card. Stick three stars on the circle and a toadstool in the bottom right-hand corner of the wine red card. Stick a border sticker around the window frame. Make a window decoration in the bottom left-hand corner from three pines, a sprig of holly and a double rose. The card is finished in the same way as described for card 1.

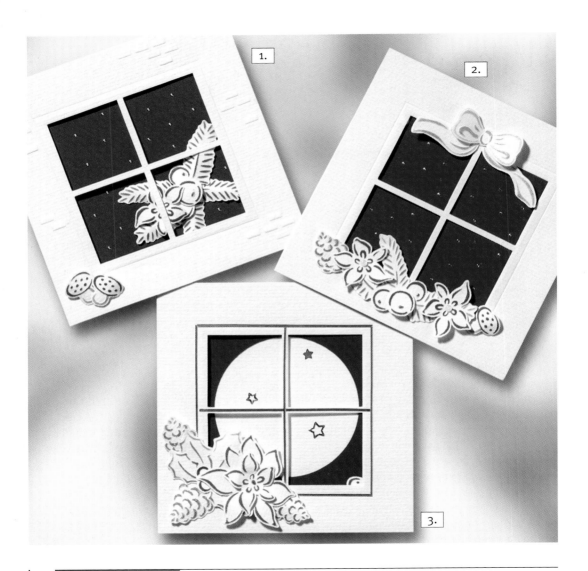

1.

2.

3.

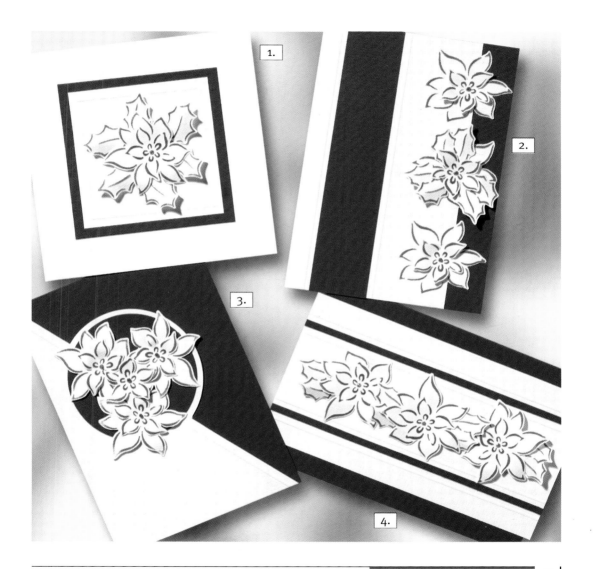

1.

2.

3.

4.

Red winter roses

The colour of the card

is reflected in the leaves

of the winter roses.

What you need:
- ❏ *Card: white no. 211 and*
  wine red no. 519
- ❏ *Line stencil: LE 2406*
- ❏ *Stamp-pad ink: red and green*
- ❏ *Scribbles: gold*

Card 1

Make a double card (12.5 x 12.5 cm) and stick
a piece of wine red card (8.5 x 8.5 cm) on it. Cut
a piece of white card (7.5 x 7.5 cm). Emboss a
border 0.5 cm from the sides (see Techniques,
tip 3) and stick it on the wine red card. Emboss
three sets of two holly leaves and a winter rose.
Stipple them before removing the stencil. Cut
everything out leaving a 2 mm border. Slightly
bend the leaves and the rose, place a drop of
silicon glue behind each one and stick them on
the card. If you wish, you can add a small drop
of gold Scribbles to the middle of the rose.

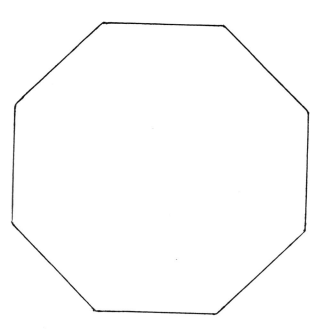

Add a drop of silicon glue behind them and stick them on the card as shown in the photograph. If you wish, add a small drop of gold Scribbles to the middle of the rose.

Card 3

This card is the same as card 3 in Winter rose, but without the background. I have added a border on both sides of the curve (see Techniques, tip 3). Emboss and stipple three winter roses and four centres and stick them on the card in a pretty arrangement. The card is finished as described above.

Card 2

Emboss three winter roses on the right-hand side of a double card. Stipple each one before removing the stencil. Make the centre of three roses and three sets of two holly leaves in the same way. Cut the individual pieces out leaving a 2 mm border. Use a ruler to cut a straight line 2 cm from the edge of the card between the roses and cut the roses out leaving a 2 mm border. Stick half a piece red card on the inside of the card and a strip of red card on the front. Slightly bend the individual pieces.

Card 4

Cut a piece of white card (15.5 x 8.5 cm). Emboss a border (see Techniques, tip 3) 1 cm and 2 cm from both edges. Stick a thin strip of red card between the borders. Stick this on a red double card. The white card will protrude 0.5 cm. Emboss and stipple three roses and four sets of two holly leaves as described above. The card is finished in the same way as described for the other cards. Stick everything on the card as shown in the photograph.

Viewing holes

Pretty viewing holes
looking out onto a white,
snowy wonder world.

What you need:
- ❏ Romak viewing hole cards
- ❏ Line stencils: LE 2403 and LE 2401
- ❏ Brown washi paper
- ❏ Aleene's True Snow

Card 1

Emboss the hills on the front of the card and emboss snowflakes around the opening. Stick a piece of torn washi paper which is slightly larger than the opening inside the card. Emboss and stipple three small trees and cut them out. Slightly bend them and stick them on the card using silicon glue. Fold the middle card closed and stick an embossed and stippled tree in the bottom right-hand corner. Note: the top half of the tree will be seen through the opening. Next, do the front of the card. Emboss and stipple a tree, a squirrel looking to the left and two squirrels looking to the right. Cut them out leaving a 2 mm border. Slightly bend the tree and stick it on the hills using silicon glue. Half of this tree will also be over the opening. Bend the squirrels into a natural shape (stomach out, tail curling outwards). Stick them around the tree using a drop of silicon glue. Add some snow to the trees and hills using a cocktail stick.

Card 2

Emboss the hills and some stars on the front of the card. Stick torn washi paper on the inside of the card. Emboss and stipple two birds and cut them out. Slightly bend them and stick them on the background. Stick a tree on the left-hand

1.

2.

3.

side of the middle card and a bird table (in 3D) with two birds on the front of the card. The card is finished in the same way as the two other cards.

Card 3

Emboss the hills on the front of the card. Cut a circle (ø 7.5 cm) out of a scrap piece of brown paper or tear it out of washi paper and stick it on the middle card. Emboss and stipple a large tree and cut it out leaving a 2 mm border. Slightly bend it and stick it on the circle using a large drop of silicon glue. Fold the middle card closed. Emboss and stipple a tree and a rabbit and cut them out. Stick the tree on the right-hand side, so that half of it is in front of the circle. Stick the rabbit to the left of the tree. Slightly bend both before sticking them on the card. Stick another rabbit on the front of the card, on the right-hand side of the hills. Add some snow to the hills using a cocktail stick.

Lanterns

Lanterns shine their light

on dark winter days.

What you need:
- ❏ *Card: white no. 211*
- ❏ *Line stencil: LE 2406*
- ❏ *Stamp-pad ink: Silver and red*
- ❏ *Christmas vellum: blue, green and red*
- ❏ *Double-sided Aslan*

Card 1

Stamp-pad ink: gold and red

For this card, cut a rectangle (8.5 x 5.8 cm) out of a scrap piece of card and use this as a stencil. Stick this in the middle of the front of a square double card using non-permanent tape. Open the card cover and emboss this shape on the inside. Inside the card, draw a pencil line from the top left-hand corner to the bottom right-hand corner. Cut away the top part of the card along the diagonal line, staying 0.5 cm from the rectangle. Emboss and stipple a lantern in the middle of the card. Make the top part of the lantern 3D. Roughly cut out three different stars from the red vellum. Stick them on double-sided Aslan and cut them out. Stick the red vellum on the inside of the card using double-sided Aslan. You can also buy this type of card.

Card 2

Cut out a strip of blue Christmas vellum (6.5 cm wide) and stick it on double-sided Aslan. Cut a very narrow strip off of this. Stick both strips on a double card as shown in the photograph. Roughly cut out a star. Stick it on Aslan and cut it out leaving a 2 mm wide blue border. Stick this in the top right-hand corner of the card. Emboss and stipple a lantern, making the top section 3D, and cut it out leaving a 2 mm border. Slightly bend the lantern and stick it on the card using silicon glue.

Card 3

On the inside of the front of a double card, draw a line from the top left-hand corner to the bottom right-hand corner. Copy the octagon (see page 19) on a scrap piece of card. Place this on the inside of the card and draw around the top half as far as the diagonal line. Cut away the top part of the card along the diagonal line, remaining 0.5 cm from the octagon. Cut the octagon out of green Christmas vellum and stick it on the front of the card. Also stick vellum to the back using double-sided Aslan. Finish the lantern as described for cards 1 and 2. You can also buy this type of card.

Frames

Various winter symbols are brought together in a frame.

What you need:
- ❏ Card: white no. 211, wine red no. 519, apple green no. 367 and royal blue no. 427
- ❏ Line stencils
- ❏ Stamp-pad ink
- ❏ Organza ribbon

Card 1

Line stencils: LE 2406 and LE 2403 •
Stamp-pad ink: gold and blue
Make a double card (17 x 9 cm) and cut out a slightly smaller piece of blue card. Cut a piece of white card (14 x 6.5 cm) and emboss a border around it (see Techniques, tip 3). Emboss and stipple three different sized stars. Emboss a bow, a tree and a squirrel on a scrap piece of card. Stipple them before removing the stencil. Cut everything out leaving a 2 mm border. Slightly bend them and stick them on the card using silicon glue.

Card 2

Line stencil: LE 2405 • Stamp-pad ink: gold and blue

Make a double card (17 x 9 cm) and stick a piece of wine red card (15 x 7 cm) on it. Cut a piece of card (13.5 x 5.6 cm) and emboss a border around it 0.5 cm from the sides (see Techniques, tip 3). Emboss and stipple some text. Stick this card on the wine red card. Emboss and stipple two Christmas bouquets on a scrap piece of card, making the holly of the bouquet 3D, and cut them out leaving a 2 mm border. Slightly bend them and raise the holly of the bouquet using silicon glue. Stick them on the card at different heights using silicon glue. Finish the card with a some Organza ribbon.

Card 3

Line stencil: LE 2406 • Stamp-pad ink: gold
Stick a piece of apple green card (10.5 x 10.5 cm) on a double card (12.5 x 12.5 cm). Cut a piece of white card (7.5 x 7.5 cm) and emboss a border around it. Emboss and stipple some text and, if you wish, a sprig of holly. Stick this card on the green card using four drops of silicon glue so that it is slightly raised. Emboss and stipple the candles and cut them out leaving a 2 mm border. Slightly bend them and stick them on the card using silicon glue. Stick a piece of Organza ribbon in the top left-hand corner.

Christmas doors

These doors invite you inside.

What you need:
- ❏ *Card: white no. 211*
- ❏ *Line stencil: LE 2405*
- ❏ *Stamp-pad ink: brown, gold, silver, blue and red*
- ❏ *Aleene's True Snow*

Card 1

Cut an A4 card lengthways through the middle and fold it double. Emboss and stipple a door 2.5 cm from the edge. Add two baskets to the left of the door at different heights. Emboss two trees and a lantern on a scrap piece of card and cut them out leaving a 2 mm border. Emboss some snowflakes around the door. Slightly bend the trees and the lantern. Place a drop of silicon glue behind them and stick them on the card. After they have dried, add some snow using a cocktail stick.

Card 2

Brick stencil (if required)
Emboss and stipple a door in the middle of the card 2 cm from the bottom edge. Emboss some bricks around the door. You can easily make a stencil if you do not have one. Cut approximately five bricks out of a scrap piece of card and use this as a stencil. Emboss and stipple a wreath (do the ribbon twice) (see Techniques, tip 2, for instructions on how to stipple the berries). Place a small drop of silicon glue behind the loops, so that they are slightly raised, and a large drop of silicon glue behind the wreath. Stick it on the door. Emboss and stipple the basket and six separate apples and cut them out leaving a 2 mm border. Slightly bend the basket. Stick it on the card and arrange the apples in it, placing a drop of silicon glue behind each apple. After they have dried, add some snow using a cocktail stick.

Card 3

This card is made according to the instructions given for cards 1 and 2.

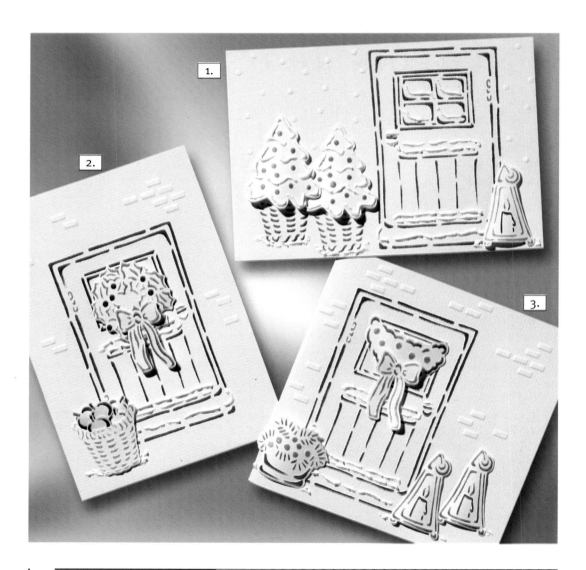

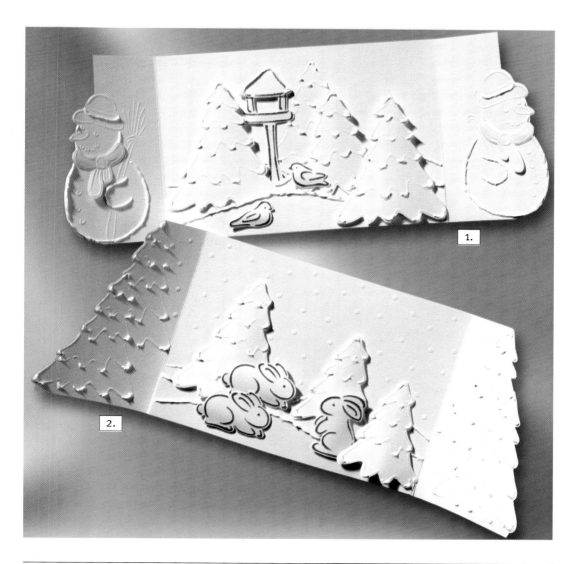

1.

2.

Christmas landscape

It is not very often that you see such a snowy white landscape.

What you need:
- ❏ *Card: white no. 211*
- ❏ *Line stencil: LE 2403*
- ❏ *Stamp-pad ink: brown and red*
- ❏ *Aleene's True Snow*

Card 1

Cut an A4 card lengthways and, on both sides, fold a 7.5 cm wide strip towards the middle. Emboss a snowman on both sides (do the scarf twice), with the nose pointing towards the outside of the card. Cut a line 4 cm from the fold almost to the hat and cut the rest of the card away leaving a 2 mm border. Emboss the highest hill straight onto the card. Emboss the two smaller hills separately on a scrap piece of card and cut them out. Emboss a tree not quite in the middle of the card and emboss three other trees on a scrap piece of card. Emboss and stipple a bird table and two birds. Cut out the individual pieces leaving a 2 mm border. Slightly bend the two separate hills. Place a large drop of silicon glue behind them and stick them on the card. Stick the outer edges of the hills to the card. Slightly bend the trees and the birds. First, stick the bird table on the highest hill using a small drop of silicon glue. Next, stick the three trees on the card at different heights on the hills using a large drop of silicon glue. Finally, add some snow using a cocktail stick.

Tip
Cut off the roof of the bird table. The middle section can then be cut away easily. Stick the roof back on using a drop of silicon glue so that it sits just over the line where it was cut off.

Card 2

Fold the card as described for card 1. Emboss a tree on both sides. Emboss another tree on top of the trees to continue the diagonal line. Cut along the outside leaving a 2 mm border. Emboss snowflakes on the middle section of the card. Emboss the hills as described for card 1. Emboss three trees and cut them out. Emboss and stipple three rabbits and cut them out. Slightly bend all the individual pieces. Stick the trees and the rabbits on the card at different heights to give the card some depth. Add some snow to the trees and hills using a cocktail stick.

Candles

The glow of the candles lights up the dark nights.

What you need:
- ❏ *Card: white no. 211*
- ❏ *Line stencil: LE 2406*
- ❏ *Christmas vellum*
- ❏ *Stamp-pad ink: gold*
- ❏ *Double-sided Aslan*
- ❏ *Organza ribbon*

Card 1

Use double-sided Aslan to stick the Christmas vellum around a square double card (12.5 x 12.5 cm). The vellum may also be loose at the back. Cut out a square (7 x 7 cm) from the front of the card. Use the cut out square as a stencil to make a frame on the background. Emboss three candles exactly in the middle of this frame. Only stipple the round parts. Emboss and stipple the candles on a scrap piece of card and cut them out leaving a 2 mm border. Slightly bend them and stick them on the background with a drop of silicon glue. Decorate the card with an Organza ribbon on the middle candle.

Card 2

Cover a double card with Christmas vellum (see card 1). Cut out a rectangle (6.5 x 5 cm) in the bottom right-hand corner 1.5 cm from the bottom and side edges. The frame and candles are made as described for card 1. Stick an Organza ribbon in the top left-hand corner of the rectangle.

Card 3

Cut an A4 card lengthways through the middle and fold it double. Cover the card with Christmas vellum using double Aslan, leaving it loose at the back. Cut a circle (Ø 7 cm) out of the front of the card. Use the cut out circle as a stencil to make a frame on the background. Make the candles as described above. Tie an Organza ribbon around the card along the line of the fold.

Thanks to Kars for providing the materials and Romak for the frame cards.

Shopkeepers can order the materials from
Kars & Co B.V., Ochten, the Netherlands • Romak B.V., Hillegom, the Netherlands (frame cards).